Special Moments

with Daddy

By Mark Garcia

Published by
Spiritbuilding Publishers
9700 Ferry Road, Waynesville, OH 45068

(800) 282–4901

SPECIAL MOMENTS WITH DADDY
by Mark Garcia

ISBN: 978–1–955285–14–8

Scripture taken from the NEW AMERICAN STANDARD BIBLE, © Copyright The Lockman Foundation 1960, 1962, 1963, 1968, 1971, 1972, 1973, 1975, 1977, 1995. Used by permission.

Spiritbuilding
PUBLISHERS

spiritbuilding.com
Spiritual equipment for the contest of life

Dedication from Mark

To my daughter Amy and my mom Trudy, both of whom have been tremendous examples to me and fine Christian ladies.

Ingrid Roskay, you are more like a big sister than an aunt to me, protecting me, teaching me, and still sharing your pearls of wisdom.

Thoughts from Amy

My Dad has been working on this book since I was a child. It was touching to read the finished product, with all the love and effort he put into it. There were several instances I didn't recall so it was worthwhile for him to save those memories for the years to come.

I hope this book will help those who feel alone as they face the challenges of life. Perhaps the experiences shared within can provide some humor and encouragement to get them through the difficult days.

Acknowledgements

Noreen MacDonald for her help and encouragement. Dr. Eva Ananiewicz and Thomas Rexrode, my life-long friends for their years of encouragement and cherished friendship.

Matthew and Becky Allen, this wouldn't be possible without you.

My love to all of you

Table of Contents

Foreward

I have known many dads and daughters from across the country, as many have attended my father-daughter retreat that I started in 2008. Mark and Amy stand out in a big way. I know them both personally, and as I read this book, I was touched at many connections of things I know personally about them, and how they intersect with things I read in the book. Mark is absolutely the kind of person who has a servant's heart. He would do anything for you, and has even helped me in a very delicate situation. Amy is the same way. They both have a massive capacity to give to others, but especially to their family and loved ones.

This book is a transparent look at the realities of life, love, and hard times, seen through the eyes of a daughter and a father who went beyond the extra mile to fight for his daughter. You will be touched, in many ways. But I guarantee you will be inspired.

Frederic Gray
Preacher, Seminole Church of Christ

Chapter 1

Sharing a Moment in Time

I will bless the Lord at all times; His praise shall continually be in my mouth.
My soul shall make its boast in the Lord; the humble shall hear it and rejoice.
O magnify the Lord with me, and let us exalt His name together.
(Psalm 34:1–3)

Close your eyes, relax, and open the treasure chest within your mind. Think back on the fondest memories of your life where you revisit those wondrous times that are as precious to you as life itself. You sense each prized instance when you almost felt Heaven's presence here on Earth.

All of us have experienced special times in our lives that we wish could have lasted forever. Recalling those delightful events is a priceless and joyous sensation to our hearts. That occasion may have been a trip to an amusement park or to the beach, glimpsing a shooting star, riding a bicycle without training wheels for the first time, a favorite birthday party or a date with our first love. In most cases those moments seemed to have been better when we had a special person with whom to share those cherished spans of time. Our thoughts focus on these periods, possibly wishing there was a way in which to stop or slow time so that we could have made them last just a little longer than they actually did. In our daydreams maybe they do. It is almost certain that they remain imprinted in our memories as a series of snapshots in the album of our lives, to be taken out and enjoyed whenever we wish to journey back to bask in the bliss of that event.

We may also come to realize that our lives are a collection of these moments in time for us to cherish. We tend to share the most precious of these intervals with those who are the closest to our hearts. Those moments are even more precious to us when we spend them with someone who is able to provide us with a broader insight into how wonderful they can be if we do not overlook them or take them for granted. We are truly fortunate if that person takes the opportunity to reveal the wonders around us that may be found in the simplest forms and levels of everyday life, to aid us in opening our hearts and minds so that we may relate our new experiences with the other wonders of life that we have yet to grasp. This awareness may be accomplished by calling to our attention moments such as the marvels of nature, our first-time achievements, results from a simple act of kindness or spending time with elderly persons listening to their first-hand stories of how things happened in the past. In revealing these wonders, they may be helping us to appreciate those precious times in a way that can and should bring pleasure to our everyday existence.

My daddy has an exceptional gift for helping people to become aware of how special they are and how we must learn to find this quality within ourselves. His example, along with his poetry, also served to remind me that, for the most part, the trials we face every day are generally circumstantial and will disappear as the fog does when the morning sun breaks through to illuminate the world around us, thereby making clear that which was once hidden.

Daddy is one of those unique people who could see things happening from a vantage point not taken by most people, and he made those instances special moments in my life as we shared them. The extraordinary relationship I had with my daddy as a child continues to this day and is described in the following pages. They are a true account of events that occurred in our lives and of how we dealt with them. Along with his poetry, the introductions are written to capture our emotions at that point in our lives. The introductions also share what inspired my daddy to write each of the poems as well as give a glimpse of our special relationship.

In an age when many parents have made families disposable by leaving spouses and sometimes children behind as if they did not exist, my daddy has been and always will be there for me. His strong nature, coupled with a big heart, brought me the love, security, and peace of mind that I needed as a child and that I can still draw from today. This book was designed for the readers' enjoyment as well as an attempt to lift their spirits through emotionally challenging periods of life that all of us face. It is intended to show one of many possible ways to have a positive outlook during trials and situations of everyday life, as well as to offer a sense of hope by the examples of how we were able to overcome the difficulties we faced together. It is also meant to be an example of the great happiness we can receive and bring to those we come in contact with throughout the course of our lives in sharing a part of ourselves with others.

"That which has been is that which will be, and that which has been done is that which will be done. So, there is nothing new under the sun" (Ecclesiastes 1:9).

The experiences described in this book are not unique in that everyone has known delight and sorrow at some time. The difference may be in how we, my daddy and I, chose to deal with those experiences and emotions by applying our faith in God. The true stories in this book show a special relationship of a father and his child. They can also demonstrate examples of the joy we receive and are able to bring to the lives of those with whom we come in contact throughout the course of our lives as we share a part of ourselves with them.

The following poem, "Sharing a Moment in Time," came about after an evening of stargazing with my daddy. We spent the early part of the night just enjoying each other's company as we watched the stars perform their unique and awesome display. *By the word of the Lord the heavens were made, and by the breath of His mouth all their host,* Psalm 33.6. That specific viewing could not have been very long since the next morning was a school day. But neither of us wanted the time we shared to come to an end. Daddy even commented that there was nowhere on earth he would rather be than right there with me. I learned much about the moon and the stars that night. However, I learned an even greater lesson: people and our relationships with them are more important than possessions. Likewise, we must make the most of our precious days with those we love by, "Sharing a moment in time." To me the moon will never be as large or the stars shine as brightly as they did that wonderful evening watching the sky with daddy.

Sharing a Moment in Time

Would the full moon seem so vast,
or the stars light shine as bright.
Can the arms of night hold fast
the advancing of daylight?
If this time could last forever,
the moment we two are near,
my love I would endeavor
to always be right here.
Nothing on earth offered me
with your presence can compare;
such pleasure would be empty
if deprived of time to share.

Chapter 2

The Proposal

Every good thing bestowed and every perfect gift is from above, coming down from the Father of lights, with whom there is no variation, or shifting shadow. In the exercise of His will He brought us forth by the word of truth, so that we might be, as it were, the first fruits among His creatures. This you know, my beloved brethren. But let everyone be quick to hear, slow to speak and slow to anger; for the anger of man does not achieve the righteousness of God, (James 1:17–20).

My daddy has always been both a hopeful romantic and an optimist, at least according to my Grandma. We all call her Ma. She told me of how he was devoted to doing kind acts for the young ladies he dated. He would also demonstrate this kindness by his willingness to stick by them no matter what their situation. In both good times and bad, he could always seem to find the silver lining to any circumstance. He was very optimistic, to the point where, instead of seeing the glass half empty, he saw the glass half full with the potential for overflowing.

Once, daddy told me a joke that was supposed to show me exactly how positive he really was. He said, "When I was a child my parents believed I was too positive. They enlisted the help of a psychologist who felt he could cure me of this supposed personality disorder. Since my birthday was in a few days, he instructed my parents to remove all of my belongings from my room and then fill the room with horse manure. Certainly, this would cause me to view the world with a less than rosy outlook. Later that day they brought me to my room. When I saw the huge pile of horse manure, I jumped into the middle of it and began to dig. My parents were completely disgusted and confused by my actions as well as my apparent delight at the situation. My father said to me, "Son, what are you doing?" I replied, "With all of this horse manure, surely there must be a pony in here somewhere!"

Daddy's optimism was especially keen when it came to believing in people whom he cared about. Daddy would always see such potential in them. It seemed strange to me that those same people almost never saw these gifts within themselves in the same way daddy did until it was pointed out to them. This may be one reason he poured so much of his love into the way he wrote all of those romantic and uplifting poems. He once told me how he sometimes had trouble saying the words he felt deep within his heart. It seemed much easier for him to write about what he felt.

He went on to say, "That reticence is because people can change the words around on a page so they express the way they feel. They can even erase those words before they have had a chance to make an impression, whether good or bad. Nevertheless, once a word has been spoken, it is impossible to change that word or the message that was sent. There is no way to unsay something. The only thing a person can do after he or she has said something is to say something else in an attempt to change or sharpen the image." "I have often regretted my speech, never my silence," is a quote from Publius, daddy told me. "We must always be very careful about choosing what it is that we say and how we say it." Daddy always reminded me to keep my speech pleasant to avoid hurting others and to look for the good qualities that exist in every individual. If you can focus your thoughts on these things, then your speech will reflect the same pleasant character. Dr. Martin Luther King once said, "Speak only well of people and you will never have to whisper."

One of daddy's first expressions through writing poems was to my mother. He called it "The Proposal" because it said in writing what he was having trouble telling her in spoken words. He asked her to marry him! He was so nervous about asking mother to marry him, but you would never know it by reading this poem! I know that much preparation went into the outpouring of his heartfelt words in this message for my mother. It expressed sentiments that come very few times in life. For many feelings, such as those he expressed in his poem, manifest themselves only once in a lifetime for some people or maybe not at all. He wanted those words to be perfect for her, and he painstakingly chose each and every word to fit their relationship. Those words would have to convey the way that things were in their lives and the way he hoped they would someday become. Each word had meaning in that it carried the message a young man in love had for the young woman he wanted to make his partner for life.

6

Daddy also wanted to make his feelings from that moment something permanent. To make this one instance in his life more tangible, he put his emotions into words, and he put the words down on paper. He desired a means by which to pass these words along through time in a special way so that others could know of his great love for my Mother. He wanted to review them with her occasionally should she accept his offer of marriage. Having a family was a serious consideration for their future. He also wanted to be able to show any children they might have exactly how special their mother and the commitment they had made to one another was to him. Daddy also realized how important it would be for their children to know how much their parents cared for one another even in the beginning of their relationship. In this way, he was able to do what few others have done. He made "The Proposal" not only a tender moment in time in which he shares his feelings of love, but also a moment everlasting for both of them.

The resulting poem, "The Proposal", shows no signs of the butterflies that were racing around within his stomach that day in those last anxious moments before he handed the poem to his future bride. It merely reflects the intensity of the emotions he had for her in the best way that he felt he could express them, through his written expression of love. It was a wonderful experience, one that I hope many others may enjoy during some time in their lives. I know that I certainly look forward to that type of a love in my life.

The Proposal

Will you give our love a chance,
and allow it grow beyond romance?
Journey with me the road to true love
that brightens the pathway to realms above.
Just as peace is to the dove
so shall our names be to love.
In this time of your decision
please go the way I envision.
A truer love cannot be
together God, you, and me.

Chapter 3
The Wedding

For this cause a man shall leave his father and his mother, and shall cleave to his wife; and they shall become one flesh (Genesis 2:24).

The marriage of the two most important individuals of my life finally took place after several minor mishaps. The rehearsal and rehearsal dinner were scheduled the night before my parents were to be wed.

The wedding took place in my mother's hometown, where most of her family still lives today. This was about sixty miles away from where daddy and his family were living at that time. As it is with many weddings, people came in from all over the country, and some of those folks participated in the wedding.

Daddy had every intention of being at the church on time for the rehearsal, but that wasn't the way it turned out. Even good intentions can be thwarted by the unfortunate circumstances of life. His younger brother had borrowed his car the morning of the rehearsal dinner, but by that afternoon he had accidentally locked the keys inside. Along with the keys he had also locked his wallet with all his money inside. This mishap took place about ten miles from where daddy was staying at that time. Several tension-filled hours passed before my uncle was able to get in touch to have him come unlock the car. This calamity took place many years before modern cellphones were available. In the meantime, my uncle tried unsuccessfully to get into the car without breaking the glass or doing any other damage. By the time they were able to get the car open, get themselves cleaned up and get on the road, they were several hours behind schedule. Phone calls to my mother's relatives were in vain because everyone was at the rehearsal site. Daddy could not remember the name of the place where they were holding this function, only how to get there. They arrived at the rehearsal about three hours late, and by that time most of the wedding party had gotten tired of waiting and had gone back home. This is not a story my uncle enjoys hearing repeated. He would be much happier if everyone just forgot the entire episode ever took place.

My mother and her family were so concerned that they had the Highway Patrol out looking for daddy because they had received no word from him. He had attempted to call their house too, but of course they were already at the church building preparing for the big event. Another problem with his being so upset was that he couldn't remember the name of the church to call them to explain.

Daddy recalled seeing looks ranging from relief to mild irritation on the faces greeting him by those folks who were still at the building. As everyone who remained took his or her places to rehearse, daddy explained to my mother what had happened to put him behind schedule. Because he was returning home that night, my mother's family suggested that it might be a good idea to have the best man drive him to the church the next day. This way there would not be any more car problems to cause any more delays. Unfortunately, the next day was when the second mishap took place.

The next morning, on their way to the wedding, the best man's car got a flat tire a few miles outside of the town. To make things worse, the best man had no spare tire to resolve their desperate situation. Luckily, they were within a short distance of a pay phone. Daddy called my mother's house and they sent her brother to rescue the stranded party. Her brother, my other uncle, took them straight to the church with time to spare.

The rest of the wedding went well. Occasionally, I will look at the wedding photos daddy saved for me and think of how wonderful my parents both looked on that day. Is there ever a time when a woman looks more beautiful than on her wedding day? Some may argue it is when a woman is with child. My mother looked so pretty, almost like an angel in her wedding dress. Everything about her seemed to be perfect. Her eyes were so brightly shining, her make-up done exactly right, every hair in place, and her smile could have lit up a dark stadium at midnight. I imagined how I would look when my turn came to be the bride.

Daddy looked like her handsome prince who had just arrived to carry her off to their castle to live happily ever after. From the photos it was the way I have pictured every fairy tale wedding.

The photos also show friends and relatives, some who are no longer alive, smiling and having a good time. I still can't get over how young everyone looked back then. Everyone appeared to be so happy that it makes me feel joyful every time I look at those photos. It is amazing the wonderful feelings one can experience from a simple photograph.

The first-time daddy ever showed me their wedding album, he pulled it out of his bedroom closet where he had been keeping it for me until I was old enough to appreciate it. I can still remember the strong emotions experienced by both of us as we began to turn each page for the first time together. For him they were pleasant memories of a time in his youth. For me this was the history of my family and my existence. No matter the difference, we both cherished the simple pleasures that those snapshots brought to us. This was also a time of healing and learning for each of us.

Daddy never wrote a poem for this occasion, but I wonder what he might have written if he had?

Chapter 4

Amy

And they began bringing children to Him, so that He might touch them; and the disciples rebuked them. But when Jesus saw this, He was indignant and said to them, "Permit the children to come to Me; do not hinder them; for the kingdom of God belongs to such as these, (Mark 10:13–14).

My childbirth, according to daddy, was a difficult labor for both of my parents. He always gets so excited when he talks about how I came into the world.

In every childbirth, there is always the remote possibility that during delivery something might go wrong. Things often do not go as expected. My birth was no exception.

In the early stages of my delivery, the doctor was concerned because he believed my umbilical cord might have been wrapped around my throat. This situation could lead to my choking and death. He frightened my parents by announcing to them this terrible news as if that was what was actually happening to me at that very moment. The doctor went on to say mother was going to have to prepare for immediate surgery to save my life. At this point daddy was hurried from the room for the medical staff to check mother more closely. During their brief separation, he went down the hall so that he could be alone to pray for both mother and me to get through this without any problems to either of us. As it turned out, the baby monitor they had on me was improperly connected. It had somehow come loose, thereby giving the false reading that I was in distress. In fact, I was doing just fine. However, the problems were not yet over.

Mother and daddy had done everything they could to prepare for the moment of my birth. They took child birthing classes and read almost everything they could get their hands on concerning child development and delivery. Daddy told me that he read of a new procedure where he could hold his cheek next to mother's belly and, by talking aloud, in time it would elicit a response from me. This talking procedure would allow me to hear his voice inside the womb and become accustomed to it. He wanted to bond with me and to have some sort of interaction with me before my birth. Talking to me that way must have done something. He said that after a couple of weeks of him practicing the process, I would respond in some way to his voice. I would either kick, or turn over, "perhaps you were just trying to get away from me when I was singing!" he joked. Whatever the case, he and I began our special relationship even before I was born.

Even after the doctors confirmed my mother's pregnancy, the idea of having a baby still seemed very dreamlike and surreal to him. To be an expectant parent of one's first child is a time of wonder and excitement. It wasn't until he found himself in the delivery room with my mother that my birth became a reality for him. After I was born and the doctor had congratulated them on having a healthy baby girl, the months of prayers, expectations, hopes, and dreams came to fruition.

At my birth, daddy recalled how I cried as the nurse was cleaning me. When he spoke to me, his voice seemed to have a calming effect as my crying slowed and eventually stopped. Being in the delivery room and assisting with all of the duties of childbirth was the climax of the entire process for him. Since my parents chose not to know my gender, it too was a surprise for them until the doctor announced, "you have a healthy baby girl!" Just knowing that I was healthy was a very moving experience for both of my parents. Their prayers had been answered in a positive way.

Once my birth was over, the anxiety of being a new parent fell upon him. Along with the new responsibilities of caring for a baby came some difficult challenges for my parents. Daddy was concerned about being a good father. What would things be like now that a baby was part of his world? He knew his life would never be the same again.

While reflecting upon that awesome experience, he would tell me he often wondered how long he would receive the unconditional love that a child is able to give. I believe I still possess that love for him. In the poem he named for me, "Amy," my daddy explains the thoughts and emotions he felt when becoming a new parent, receiving the type of love that a child must give.

Amy

Ever since the birth of my Amy
no greater joy has come to me.
The simple love that she has shown
until now only Heaven has known.
Blessed am I to have a daughter
as she reminds me of my mother.
Though I may not possess a thing
I'm made to feel just like a king.
I'll ask for nothing from above
but to always have my Amy's love.

Chapter 5

Good-bye to Love

"For I hate divorce," says the Lord, the God of Israel (Malachi 2:16).

When a healthy relationship is no longer possible, how does someone say, "Good-bye to Love"? This is a question that numerous people have been asked and very few can answer in such a way as to be accepted by all others. Even my daddy had to struggle with the emotions and difficulties that this question brought to him one day.

Daddy had been blessed with everything he wanted and needed in life, or so he thought. To him, his had been a storybook romance and marriage. With him as the dashing prince and his new bride, my mother, as the lovely princess. After their wedding they experienced the joy filled lives of newlyweds. Both of them had stable jobs that they enjoyed, along with nice cars, a house, an abundance of friends, and an active lifestyle full of love for one another. In addition to all of that, approximately three years after their lives as a married couple began, they found out that I was to be born. This birth, would be the beginning of a new family and yet another new lifestyle.

They both worked together to bring me into this world, more so perhaps than most couples, because of the unusual birth circumstances. Daddy played a more active physical role than most fathers have to do in a normal birthing process. Finally, I arrived as a healthy baby girl. For him, this was heaven on earth, and his life could not have been any better. He was on top of the world with his wife and new baby girl.

Sadly, my parents joy filled lives as a couple were not to last for much longer. All of the happiness that they knew from their being together would soon be coming to an end. A little over a year after I was born, things in the lives of my parents suddenly took a dramatic change for the worse.

Unfortunate and uncontrollable matters drove a wedge between my parents, one that even their love for each other could not prevent from the eventual destruction of their happiness and the wonderful times they had built together. The effects of this happening changed every aspect of their association. What had once been a beautiful relationship began to slip away into something strange and then tragically awful. The most disheartening part may have been that there was nothing anyone could have done to correct this problem. Although he had been determined to stick to his marriage vows and spend the rest of their lives together, it was not meant to be. A divorce decree was filed and what had started out as a storybook marriage soon ended, as so many marriages do, in court and then with the couple bitterly going their separate ways.

Daddy endured the torment that countless others have suffered as he was forced to salvage what he could from their hopelessly broken relationship. He had to keep going, to pull it all together, despite the immense personal pain he was experiencing. "My divorce and subsequent custody battle were the darkest, most depressing times in my life, but they taught me many things," He later remarked as he took with him whatever lessons the pain of a failed love and an ill-fated marriage presented. It reminded him of a quote by Charles A. Beard: "When it is dark enough, you can see the stars." Daddy went on to say there are times when you can do nothing about your circumstances but to be patient and appreciate those around you.

Once again, to find any positive aspects of this terrible situation, my daddy realized he had come away from his marriage with more than he had when he entered. He now had a wonderful young daughter to care for and consider. Caring for my new needs and our future together became his primary focus and responsibility. In this way, he underwent the necessary details that at that point seemed to be mundane. He settled the issues of finance and estate that always seem to be dragged through the courts when a former husband and wife go their separate ways. He had little time to feel sorry for himself or his unwanted situation as he prepared himself mentally for a new more important battle, the battle for my custody.

With all that he had been blessed with in life and then all that he had lost, it would have all been in vain to him if he had allowed this injustice to continue along that course. He was painfully aware that there was nothing that could be done to correct the mistakes of the past. By the end of all the court battles, daddy had given up most of his worldly possessions to pay for the astronomical attorney fees and doctors bills created by their divorce and subsequent custody battle. He believed there was a more important issue at stake at that moment. Knowing in his heart that I would be better off if he was the primary guiding parental force in my upbringing, and with my welfare as his objective, he knew what he had to do, and he did it. He would fight for my custody. Even though all of his closest friends as well as the first attorney he hired all said his case was hopeless, he fought for and won custody of me. A man winning custody was something totally unheard of in 1991, especially winning custody of an opposite sex child. Daddy fired his first attorney the day after he said they would not win. He later hired someone who believed in what daddy was fighting for, the best possible life for me.

It was during this time that he recognized he had mistakenly taken for granted that he would be married for the rest of his life. The idea of being divorced or even living without my mother had never entered his mind. He saw the two of them as being like milk and chocolate syrup combining to make chocolate milk. How could the two ever be separated once together? Certainly, daddy had to wonder, what does one do when those dreams of living happily ever after are shattered, and how does one handle the disturbing reality of those dreams coming to an end?

How exactly does someone deal with the end of such an emotional relationship and say "Good-bye to Love?" Anyone having lost someone whom they love can relate to this unpleasant question. My daddy examined that disorienting predicament in his poem by the same name. He made a diligent effort to find some answers that would satisfy his desire to know why this tragedy had happened to them. He once again attempted to put into words the severe pain that he felt at the end of his marriage to my mother in his poem, "Good-bye to love."

Good-bye to Love

Torn from the arms of love, how shall I endure?
For what was once a beautiful pair, are now two . . . separate.
Time, the noble healer, has abandoned me to anguish.
Our former love, like sand in an hourglass, has run out.
My tears, like rain falling on an ocean, will go unnoticed.
Loneliness has become my only companion.
Thoughts of us, once gingerly caressed, are changed forever.
All that remains, is to say,
Good-bye to Love.

Chapter 6

Loneliness

In my distress I called upon the Lord, and cried to my God for help; He heard my voice out of His temple, and my cry for help before Him came into His ears (Psalm 18:6)

When I was older, daddy explained to me how divorce has a disturbing way of driving away the best of friends. Even some of the people who were once close to him, for whatever reason, seemed to distance themselves. His circumstances must have felt awkward to his old friends who may not have known about divorce from personal experience. Although they may have meant well, to most of them, his new situation left them in a position of not knowing what to do or what to say. He thought about how married couples do not have the same things in common with someone who is single, separated, or divorced. For a period of time, even in cases where singles are still invited to functions with married couples, singles may feel out of place being the only person there without a spouse or special someone. Quite often it isn't long before the invitations stop coming.

Once his marriage ended, daddy tried to ease his loneliness by keeping himself busy all the time to prevent him from dwelling on his problems. The key, he thought, was not to allow his mind time to dwell on his unfavorable condition until he was ready and able to deal with it in a healthy manner. He reminded himself that healing was slowly coming, but meanwhile he needed to prepare himself for eligibility in the dating scene when the time was right.

The type of person he should date would be a problem for him. He found that although single people have a similar dating status, they often have a completely different agenda. Single people can sometimes have trouble relating to the priorities of the single parent. The needs of a young child must come first, and those needs sometimes require a great deal of time. A responsible single parent is not free to go wherever they please whenever they please. Daddy made me feel secure by reminding me I have always been and always will be very important in his life.

Even when dating another single parent, who can understand and relate to the nature of having a child to care for? Difficulties still arise. One of the obstacles may be how the children of both families interact. That factor alone can be cause for a relationship to end.

Another situation involving the children is the timing, as to when the children should be introduced to the person one is dating. Daddy was aware of how children can develop an attachment to a person and find it difficult to understand break ups.

The question of when a couple will be able to meet with each other can be another difficult one to answer when one or both people have a child. Trying to find the time for a courtship while they are juggling their other family responsibilities is a challenge to new relationships.

Daddy also had to consider what the effect of his past relationship might have on his future relationships. As he wrestled with the uncertainties of trying to find someone new, it was only natural for him to think about what could have happened if the old relationship had survived. Thoughts of "what if" joined themselves to his loneliness. These thoughts, allowed his mind to create little melodramas of his past relationship to my mother working into a "happy ending." Closure came when he finally accepted the reality of the past relationship, his marriage, being over, and he was able to go on with his life. It was an anxious and scary time of self-examination for him. During this period of his life, daddy was full of insecurity and self–doubt. The course he had once set for his future had been seriously altered in a way that was unwanted as well as unexpected.

Times such as this can be dark and lonely for any single parent. It certainly seemed to be a dark and troubled period. For a time, he felt as though he was completely alone except for his relatives who were supportive of him. Once, I overheard him saying he did not know how he would have gotten through this time of trial in his life if it were not for God, his relatives, and a good sense of humor. It was rare for me to ever hear him complain about his situation in life. Daddy usually tried to shelter me from those times and other adult issues that young children are not ready to face. However, when he did mention distressful situations, he usually would say "This is just situational, and that, this too will pass." In this way, he allowed me to catch a glimpse of the not so pretty side to life, and he gave me a sense of comfort that all would soon be as it should for both of us. He explained how situational issues in life are just speed bumps to keep us from senselessly flying too quickly through life. We all need to slow down and appreciate what is going on around us whether good or bad because there are lessons to be learned.

Eventually all of us must adjust in some way to the challenges that life brings to us every day. Certain compromises are usually made and a balance is achieved. A particular dating role was established that worked for both him and me. A new understanding arose that helped to solve the complications of the past and set guidelines for the future. While the idea of marriage was postponed until a much later time, it was generally understood by both of us that his being single was not a permanent condition. There was still hope for marriage and a family life for us again in the future!

While loneliness was not preferred, it was far more acceptable than the misery of staying in a sick relationship that would only bring pain. His belief was that it is better to be lonely wishing for a relationship than to be in a bad relationship wishing you were alone. Of course, his desire was to be in neither of those two circumstances. The most important thing to remember is, for Christians, joy should come from within and be something we produce rather than expecting that you will be made joyful by someone else. . It was Paul who said, *Not that I speak from want, for I have learned to be content in whatever circumstances I am. I know how to get along with humble means, and I also know how to live in prosperity; in any and every circumstance I have learned the secret of being filled and going hungry, both of having abundance and suffering need. I can do all things through Him who strengthens me,* Philippians 4.11–13. With this thought in mind, he decided once again to express his ideas and feelings by putting them into poetry. In his poem "Loneliness," daddy describes his feelings of loneliness with its faults, its mysteries, and its revelations.

Loneliness

Loneliness resembles the bitter cold
as young hearts prematurely growing old.
We become wearied by the childish games,
remembering faces, but forgetting names.
A love who has come and gone.
Having left that time, we carry on.
Was knowledge gained from those past mistakes
of our prolonged time spent in heartaches?
If badly coupled means only squabble
"then I'm better off lonely than miserable."

Chapter 7
Prepare for Love

But now abide faith, hope, love these three; but the greatest of these is love.
(1 Corinthians 12:13)

After the divorce, daddy was thrown into a whole new world of confused emotions and uneasy situations. He was free, in a sense, and open to discovering new relationships and experiences. However, he began to wonder exactly how he should prepare himself for all that comes with these new situations. It was a period in his life when he felt as if there was nothing left of himself of any value with which to start over. He struggled emotionally with his personal torment of trust issues and self-doubt. What could he have done differently? What corrections and adjustments needed to be made at that point within his life? He wanted to make this a positive learning experience that would result in something good in both of our lives.

Though I loved him very much, I was still a young child at that time and could not have advised him of what to do or even given an intelligent opinion. I hardly understood the situation as it was, having my parents in different places! This was a time when he would have to find the answers he sought by himself. Poor daddy was on his own with this one.

Where had all his previously high self-esteem gone? Most of it had probably been devoured, absorbed by the divorce decree. This feeling of low self-esteem was something he never expected, and was definitely not prepared for. What was left of his battered self-esteem was stripped away in the terrible custody battle that followed. It was not long after that when he began to question himself. He wrestled with the insecurities that followed in those types of situations. He pondered, "if I did not feel I was good enough for myself, then how could I be good enough for anyone else?" It was a question that daddy allowed to nag at him for only a short time before doing something to correct the situation.

Daddy had become his own worst critic. He seemed to be severely tested by these unyielding challenges. Just as pressure applied to a chunk of coal changes the coal into a valuable diamond, so too my daddy would come out of the pressures of those circumstances a better person for what he had gone through, and he realized that to be true when those struggles were completed.

Later in life he was able to pass on this knowledge to others as well as to me in the hopes that we could learn from his mistakes and experience without having to pay the same price he did. Hesitation is not always a bad idea when it comes to commitment, but it should be for the right reasons and not because of issues haunting us from our past.

What he believed would be the answer to his romantic situation appeared unexpectedly. As often seems to be the case when we stop looking for love, it comes looking for us. There was an opportunity opened to him. It was a lady whom he both respected and for whom he felt a strong attraction. She was a wonderful person, his dream come true, good to both daddy and me. I remember her being kind, smart, pretty, and most of all, lots of fun. But he could not get beyond the still present pain and trust issues he suffered from his divorce. He feared trusting and loving someone again, only to be hurt once more. He did not wish to go through with this lady the anguish that he had just been through. In this case, his fears were without any grounds, but they caused him to hesitate and question certain things about this new relationship that normally he would not have given a second thought. His hesitation and fear cost him the opportunity he may have had at making a lasting relationship with her. Unfortunately for us, she moved on with her life and daddy lost his opportunity with her forever.

With his heart still sore from before, daddy would have to deal with a new wound and, ironically, this was exactly the situation he had tried to avoid in the first place. Sometimes in our efforts to control love, we get swept aside. Now he could only imagine what a wonderful relationship he might have had with this lady if he had been able to return the love that was offered him instead of giving into his fear and hesitation.

How does someone deal with the sharp sting of wondering what might have been? This problem was yet another in a series of harsh lessons for him to learn. He decided at that point to redefine himself, along with his expectations. It was time to heal completely before moving on with his love life. He regained his self-esteem and prepared for a time when the next opportunity would present itself. He would never again lose a chance for a relationship that might develop into something more because of his fear or hesitation.

Armed with this newly found knowledge and courage, soon after his healing process was completed, daddy was ready for love to begin again for him. However, this time he was not chained to his past. His healthy and lighthearted approach seemed to be more appealing and successful.

In the poem "Prepare for Love," daddy reveals the feelings and thoughts that led him to close an old troubled chapter in his life and create a new healthy one. His renewal in life opened doors to him for a wonderful world of fresh opportunities and ideas. It was a new start for both of us as well as a big step in our lives together, as we both began to "Prepare for Love."

Prepare for Love

I envisioned her once, but I was not quite sure.
In a daydream I had she appeared so demure.
My heart began racing, hesitating I erred.
When an opportunity appeared, I was not yet prepared.
In a moment it passed, and my heart was broken.
The message was clear, though no words were spoken.
Cupid is impatient, and for whom shall he wait?
If I am not ready, then for me it's too late.

Chapter 8
The Land of Your Imagination

And He called a child to Himself and stood him in their midst, and said,
"Truly I say to you, unless you are converted and become like children,
you shall not enter the kingdom of heaven" (Matthew 18:2–3).

When I was a little girl, I can remember a favorite pastime that daddy and I used to play together after a rainstorm. It was something so simple, and to others it may have even seemed silly, but to us it was brimming with good times filled with magic and adventure. After a heavy rain, daddy and I would go outside and begin a search of the grounds next to our home for pebbles. Not just any pebbles. These were the tiny river rocks that were sometimes used by builders on houses for roofing. Summer storms in Florida brought heavy rain that would break a small number of those pebbles loose each time and wash these little rocks from our roof. They were mostly off white in color but a few were other colors as well. Some of them were black, gray, brown, and orange. A very few of those appeared to be bronze. We picked up all of these tiny rocks, but the bronze-colored pebbles were the ones we were in search of. To us the bronze-colored rocks were of great value, the kind of stones that were a real prize, our treasure to be carried away and later displayed.

To me as a child this was not a task of clean up; rather, it was a treasure hunt. In fact, the truth of the matter was that the treasure we had was far more precious than those little trinkets. It was how, with his wonderful imagination, daddy was able to create a fantastic memory and a bond that will stay with me forever. Those special moments we shared will always be the real treasure for both of us. Through his example, something that in time I hope to pass on to my children, daddy showed me that the true treasures in life are people, not money or things.

Often, after our energetic treasure hunt, we would relax from our labors by lying next to each other in the grass which by that time had dried from the sunshine. As we were lying there in the quiet comfort of our backyard, we would watch the clouds now peacefully floating up above us as they shifted from one pattern into another. What we each saw varied every time we played this simple game. We would take turns pointing at a cloud and calling out to each other what we saw in the shapes of those billows. One moment I imagined there was a kitten; in the next, the kitten had become a rabbit; then it was a horse, and just before it blew away, it became a bird. Each time we would play this game, the clouds somehow became something more extraordinary as my mental abilities grew.

I was always amazed at daddy's reaction to what I envisioned the clouds to be. He seemed to take such an interest in what those white puffs meant to me and how my imagination grew. He told me that at times like this he felt as if I brought back the kid in him. It helped him to recall the memories of a time in his past when he would share special moments with his father. He credited my grandfather with being the person most responsible for him being the great parent that he turned out to be. His daddy was a fine example of a parent from the time my Daddy was a boy until he became a man. He also said that he tried his best to be the parent God wanted him to be to fulfill the great responsibility he had been given as a parent. God, our heavenly Father, is the best example of how to be a successful parent.

Ask, and it will be given to you; seek, and you will find; knock, and it will be opened to you. For everyone who asks receives, and he who seeks finds, and to him who knocks it will be opened. Or what man is there among you who, when his son asks for a loaf, will give him a stone? Or if he asks for a fish, he will not give him a snake, will he? If you then, being evil, know how to give good gifts to your children, how much more will your Father who is in heaven give what is good to those who ask Him! (Matthew 7.7–11)

While we enjoyed these times as fun exercises of our imaginations and as quality time together, it was also a time of learning for both of us. It was a time when we each learned how important our imaginations can be as well as how much these quality times meant. When I was older, daddy explained to me the importance of keeping my imagination alive in the experiences life brought my way. By keeping your imagination alive one can add a new dimension not only to ones' imagination but also to ones' experiences. He went on to say, "Never be afraid to use your imagination or to see the world through the eyes of someone else. By doing so, you might be surprised at the new appreciation that you have for the world around you."

Daddy shared with me that as a young boy he was able to look at three small, discarded wheels on the side of a road and think to himself, there is the beginning of my new go-kart. His imagination would allow him to picture what the result was before he even got close enough to the wheels to see that they were already worn out and good for nothing but the trash heap they sat in. The worn-out wheels did not prevent him from having the same excited reaction the next time he saw a discarded lawn mower, which would soon be the engine he needed for his go-kart.

We all need to be reminded of those times when our imaginations were allowed to run free, to grow strong, entertain us, and in some cases be our only companions. We can drift back to a time when our dreams were as real and fantastic to us as the hope of them possibly coming true someday. In today's world, being an adult can be a hard way to go without a little playtime. Some adults have allowed their lives and imaginations to go from being adventuresome to that of inactivity. What a terrible loss for them!

We live in a world where people are constantly challenged to defend their thoughts, actions, opinions, and desires. Conformity has become the word of the day with some folks. Is it any wonder then those adults seem to be so closed minded and skeptical about the world around them? Things that were once bright and colorful to them in their childhood have in their later years become drained into a dull black and white with occasional shades of gray. The answer to this problem may be that adults need to find the rainbow existing inside of us all that brings back the beauty, joy, playfulness, and vividness of their childlike inner thoughts, hopes, and dreams. It was Jesus who said, *I have come as Light into the world, so that everyone who believes in Me will not remain in darkness,* John 12:46.

Those special yesterdays can once again be taken with them to help in creating their special tomorrows in a land where hopes and dreams still live. It is only when adults fill themselves with this rainbow of colors through opening their minds and imaginations that they can hope to find what they have lost somewhere along the road to becoming an adult. By looking to the clouds, one may grasp the simple fun in life. By looking inside, one may find the treasure that lies in every relationship that is built.

In the poem titled "The land of your imagination," daddy has expressed a desire to do just that. He captures one of our cloud gazing moments, and in it has made me see the guiding light that brings us all to a purer, simpler, more pleasant time. It gives me hope in the idea that the wonderful world as seen through the eyes of a child does not have to be limited to children. It can go on past our childhood for as long as we keep our hearts young. We need not be children to see the wonders this world has to offer and appreciate them every day. That incredible journey can begin by the simple act of gazing at a passing cloud or by merely looking into the wondrous eyes of a child for guidance in finding your way back to the land of imagination.

The Land of Your Imagination

What do you see when you gaze at a cloud?
What seems clear to you, to me, has a shroud.
Help me to stretch beyond my limited reach,
to explore the concepts only you can teach.
Take me to a land where imaginations can grow.
A place where rivers of dreams still flow.
A time mixed with yesterdays and tomorrows,
heaped with happiness, and void of all sorrows.
Where a child's thoughts will always race.
Won't you guide me to this magical place?

Chapter 9
My Sunshine

For as he thinks within himself, so he is (Proverbs 23:7).

Some daddies can fix things with tools, but mine was able to fix most things with his written words. When I was feeling upset because of harsh things someone had said to me in anger, he was capable of using his words to lift me back up. The following factual incident is but one of many times in my life that show how his words were able to help me to rise from feeling discouraged and angry to once again reaching a level of feeling special and loved.

I can remember an event that nearly broke my heart. While I was away from home, visiting another member of my family, those folks called a family meeting. One person I trusted, and the other one I did not. During this time, it came out again that this part of my family was not quite functioning in the healthy manner that they should. This dysfunction became very apparent to me during an explosion of jealous anger when he verbally attacked me. It would be truly amazing if their neighbors did not hear every word that was screamed at me, even though I was only inches away from that person's face at the time I was being severely scolded. Because I was brought up to show respect to adults, I fought back the powerful urge to tell them what I truly thought and had been feeling for some time, a feeling that they were behaving horribly and were an embarrassment to me. This was made worse by the betrayal I felt. The one who should have stood up for me and protected me from such abuse failed. Such things should never be spoken to an adult, much less a little child.

The anger I felt toward them began to burn like a fire inside my tiny body, a fire that felt as if it could have consumed me at that very moment. My little world seemed to be sinking into a pit of rage that was caused by their hideous behavior. My first thought was, "What could I have possibly done to deserve the sort of treatment I had just received?" Those words had caused me to feel so angry, so sad, so confused, and so hurt, but I held the tears inside and refused to cry or show my pain in front of them. It was some time later that day when the truth and my tears revealed themselves.

Daddy had come to pick me up after that frightful visit. During our long drive back home, I found that I could not hold my distress in any longer. I tried to act brave and behave the way I thought a grownup would by keeping the hurt inside, but soon the pain was too much as tears filled my eyes and made their way down my cheeks. He noticed this drastic change from the joy I had expressed in first seeing him, to one of hurt, and he quickly pulled the car to the side of the highway. Concerned by my tears, he asked me in a saddened and sympathetic voice what was wrong. I shared everything that happened, talking through the hurt and embarrassment I felt from the incident. He listened patiently, quietly taking in all I had to say. The more I talked through the terrible experience, the better I felt. He asked a few questions after I had an opportunity to tell my story. I was not in trouble with him. I knew I could trust him. It was some time later that I learned it took all of his self-control to keep the car on the road, to continue going home, to keep from turning the car around and confronting the offenders face to face right then. Doing that would not be the proper way to handle such a problem. *Be angry, and yet do not sin; do not let the sun go down on your anger,* Ephesians 4:26.

His protective anger was stronger even than my own, though he himself had not gone through that vulgar tongue-lashing. He bore his painful burden in silence, his own agony held inside so as not to make my pain even worse by reopening that wound and by involving children in adult issues. He quieted my tears then and there and eased the sharp stinging pain I felt so deeply within my heart. He reassured me of my value. Once again, I felt safe and at ease. While that might have been enough for some parents, daddy was not through. At the proper time and in the proper way, he addressed the incident in a manner that assured the situation would never be repeated. The legal system was not tolerant of this situation, especially when one of the two adults confessed that my story was entirely true.

Since the time of that heart-breaking situation, I have occasionally thought about the children's saying: "sticks and stones may break my bones, but words can never hurt me." In my opinion, this would be more accurate if children were to say, sticks and stones may break our bones, but hateful words can hurt us more. You may heal a broken bone in a few months but emotional scars can last for years.

Later daddy took the pain, his and mine, and in his own nurturing way was able to reshape all that had happened into something positive. He changed the pain we felt into inspiration and made that inspiration permanent in a poem, which he shared with me. It is the one he titled, "My Sunshine." He once again used his compassion and skills to change my pain into an expression of his love. He made that expression into something I could see with my eyes and touch with my hands all the way to my soul. I now have that inspirational piece and someday I can give this poem to someone else who needs the encouragement that those beautiful words gave to me during a troubling time and that continue to uplift me today.

For as long as I can remember, daddy has called me his Sunshine. He said it is because I brighten up every part of his existence. The poem My Sunshine has always helped to brighten every part of my life. This poem is but one example of the expressions of love through words, the tools, which he used to lift me above the noise of those harsh words and unpleasant feelings to see my own self-worth more clearly. My simplest acts are able to bring pleasure, to brighten his heart, and to show that I do make a positive difference to him and to this world where things are not always very pleasant. Now I smile as I look to the future.

My Sunshine

You are as special as the sun.
Your playfulness makes our lives fun.
When adversity causes brief sorrow,
your smile brings hope in tomorrow.
Adoring eyes and lips that flatter,
at no time think you don't matter.
Though some folks may fail to see it,
at times they bruise your gentle spirit.
Days are bright with joys you impart,
by the warm glow from your kind heart.
I shall recite this endlessly,
my little girl is the world to me.

Chapter 10

The "Arthurian Trilogy" on Chivalry

This is pure and undefiled religion in the sight of our God and Father, to visit orphans and widows in their distress, and to keep oneself unstained by the world (James 1:27).

There is one lady who is probably most responsible for inspiring the feelings which led to writing the following trilogy of poems although they are not necessarily about her. These poems take many references from the legend of King Arthur and the display of chivalry made by King Arthur and his Knights of the Round Table. My daddy was always striving to be chivalrous, but he appeared to be more so during times when he believed people to be in need or were distressed. He believed that his chivalry stemmed from a passage he had read in the Bible many years earlier. Proverbs Chapter 31 is generally referred to as the chapter about the "Worthy Woman". However, a few verses preceding that section instruct us to *open your mouth for the dumb, for the rights of all the unfortunate. Open your mouth, judge righteously, and defend the rights of the afflicted and needy*, Proverbs 31:8–9. Isaiah instructs us to, *cease to do evil, learn to do good; seek justice, reprove the ruthless, defend the orphan, plead for the widow*, Isaiah 1:16–17.

The first poem in this trilogy was written to a woman whom he loved who was facing some serious problems soon after her divorce. However, as in the story of Arthur and Guinevere, this love affair did not have the happy ending that one might imagine. What he thought would be a romance quickly became very rocky and then impossible. Daddy saw so much potential in this relationship and so many positive things in the beginning. As with every relationship, in time things eventually changed for the two of them, unfortunately this change was for the worse.

What really appealed to me about their relationship, was the fact that the lady had two small children about my age. Being an only child had some advantages but I had always wished for brothers and sisters. Now it appeared as though my wish was coming true. I would finally have siblings with whom I could share, play, spend time, and make memories. But the children this lady had were not the siblings of whom I had spent many hours daydreaming. They were defensive around my daddy and me. Whenever we got together her children made me feel as if I was the odd man out by refusing to play with me, or they would be very mean to me. Teasing me, annoying me, or hurting me seemed to be their dysfunctional way of relating. Daddy had not seen their bad conduct before, but when he did see it, he put a stop to it. He explained they were worried about us taking their mother away from them; and that he also believed that they would become more pleasant as they grew more comfortable with both of us. This change in behavior never happened, so when he came to me the morning after he decided not to see her any longer, I was both sad and relieved. Sad that he had not found the woman of his dreams, yet at the same time relieved that I would no longer have to endure those two little monsters.

Earlier in his relationship with this lady, daddy wrote "Guinevere, Camelot shall not fall" as a way of inspiring the woman through her tough times. He attempted to do this by explaining that these challenging times she was facing were circumstantial and that he would be there to support her in any way he possibly could. He wanted to encourage her to keep going and to hold her head high as those tough times would eventually pass. The poem worked! She was both pleased and in awe that she should inspire someone to write for her out of such deeply seated caring. She did not have many people in her life treat her the way daddy had, and I think this must have somehow disturbed her. Unfortunately, she was the type of person who always saw a glass half empty instead of half full. His attraction to her may have been one where he could come to her aid in some gallant fashion. Although romantic, rescuing this lady was not realistic or healthy for either of them. The lesson he soon learned was that he could neither have solved all of her problems nor should he have tried. The poem did however bring her great joy at that time through its positive message of hope and support. It may be that in some small way, possibly through his poetry, he was successful in his efforts to help her.

"The Death of Chivalry" was written shortly after they stopped seeing each other. The breakup was a troubling time. For a while, he questioned his beliefs about chivalry. He began to wonder if it had a place in the world today. Opening doors for ladies as well as the elderly, coming to the rescue of the weak, aiding those in need or the less fortunate, having high ideals and morals appeared to be the ways of the past. He wondered if these things would soon fade from this world completely. After all, he thought, no one ever hears of people helping people any more. It seemed to him that man's injustice toward his fellow man was the only thing that made the news. Anyone who wants to help others is unjustly labeled "codependent."

After much soul searching, he regained his perspective and decided that chivalry was not an outdated idea as long as those few who still practiced it held its truth within their hearts even if they go unappreciated by the recipients and by the rest of this world. The true reward is in doing something good for the sake of doing good. Daddy quickly recovered from the pain and disappointment he had suffered in that ill-fated relationship. Soon he was his former self, and chivalry was alive and well again in both his thoughts and deeds.

"Love for Guinevere" was a poem he wrote soon after reflecting on his relationship with that woman. He thought about past relationships and fantasized about another lady from his past, someone whom he reluctantly never dated. They were young and had somehow drifted apart.

Daddy realized how he almost let the dysfunctional relationship he had just come out of taint his views of life and love. He feared that he might grow old having no partner to complement his life in the way he hoped and intended to complement hers. Thoughts of his boyhood sweetheart made him determined not to give up hope. Those ideas helped him to realize that his dreams of loving someone and being happy were still possible. Although his childhood sweetheart was now married, they are still friends to this day.

Daddy has not given up on his quest to find true love and he has retained the use of one of his favorite sayings. I remember he mentioned the creation of this saying, which became one of his favorite phrases, was a result of the dysfunctional relationship he had with that woman. The saying went like this, "I would rather be lonely than miserable, but I wish to be neither." I hope he does find the lady of his dreams some day and that I am there to share with him all the joys that a healthy relationship such as that can bring.

The Death of Chivalry?

Weary from combat a knight does retreat.
His valiant efforts culminated in defeat.
On this day the victory has gone to another.
The willful youth was no more than a bother.
Who has dealt him this near fatal blow,
a dragon perhaps or some foreign foe?
More dangerous by far is the fair maiden,
whose heart this knight has failed to win.
Can a mere man change the course of love,
or is this a task for the angels above?
Gallantry's stronghold was in this knight's heart.
But alas, chivalry's end has come in part.
Has it passed from this world for eternity?
Or shall it be reborn anew within me?

Guinevere, Camelot Shall Not Fall

Guinevere, Camelot shall not fall
Though turmoil encompasses us now
Our solace bids good times arrival

While this chivalrous man does survive
My heart will hold a sanctuary
Where morals and ideals shall thrive

Guinevere, Camelot shall not fall
While there are ladies such as yourself
Men like me will ever give our all

I may at times topple from my stead
But mounted firmly is where I'll be
In your every hour of want or need

Guinevere, Camelot shall not fall
While the beauty of your smiling face
Is here to rejuvenate us all

A kingdom without wants or sorrow
Where we can achieve our hopes and dreams
Is but to gaze at our tomorrow

Guinevere, Camelot shall not fall
Yes, I may be a dreamer of sorts
Yet our kingdom will have no rival

Love for Guinevere

How did my life get this way,
and remain sad until today?
Awful choices I have made
with them Camelot and honor fade.
My love, can I fix these things,
the time, the place, the feelings?
Return the springtime of my life,
gentle Guinevere, my wife.
Allow for this wound to heal.
Your forgiveness is my appeal.
Guinevere return to me,
feel my state of urgency,
and my tortured heart within.
I beg that you forget my sin.
This punishment that I do pay,
by living without you each day,
is more than my soul can bare,
should I find that you don't care.
Though dim my sight, may I see
the one I love come near to me.
How much longer must I yearn
for my true love to return?
She might if she heard my plea,
to make right this tragedy.
Now she sees me at my best.
A noble man above the rest.
Life is as a fresh bouquet.
Guinevere is back to stay.

Chapter 11

My Quest for Love

Consider it all joy, my brethren, when you encounter various trials, knowing that the testing of your faith produces endurance" (James 1:2–3).

If timing is the answer, then fast may not be a sensible pace for one who is seeking true love. True love should not be rushed or forced into a compact time schedule. Rather, it may come in time, with patience and understanding. According to my daddy, he believed that in preparing for that eventful moment, the person should make him or herself ready and await love with patience.

He seemed to be very patient in his quest for a new romance. It was his intent to discover a lady for a long-term relationship who would complement his life in every way as he hoped and intended to do to hers. He knew from his past experiences that this sort of thing would take a while to develop. This situation reminded him of a time in his youth when he was not so patient, and it gave him another opportunity to share with me an important lesson based on his experience.

Out of all the lessons in life that daddy tried to help me understand, love may have been the most difficult. It is something that so many people crave but seem to have little knowledge on how to obtain it. For some, love hits them hard and fast; while for others, feelings grow stronger slowly over a period becoming love. How can we know when it is real or right for us?

There are also many different types of love: platonic, romantic, paternal, religious: other types include the love of friends, the love of pets, love of our interests—the list goes on. How could anyone, especially a young person such as I was then, be expected to sort through all of this confusion to see the true make up of love? There seemed to be an endless array of options, all leading to more questions. How does one know what love is or even if what we are experiencing is truly love? Each of us must individually search for the answer to this question as it applies to us specifically, which becomes our quest for love.

My own quest for answers about love was just beginning. I had very few experiences to compare to determine just what it was that I wanted or needed in a healthy relationship. Daddy however, had developed a life-long journey filled with a multitude of experiences in his quest for love. He had even studied books on the subject in order to help him with his decisions. He shared with me some stories of his failures as well as some of his successes in love to help me to learn and to possibly avoid similar pitfalls.

As a young man daddy began to develop his ideas of love from youthful romantic fantasies, the type that seem to fill the head of every young inexperienced person at some time in their lives. Whenever he saw a young lady in whom he was interested in pursuing in a relationship, he became excited and impatient, wishing that the new relationship he had just established would instantly flourish into what we see on TV or in movies. He would express everything he thought he felt for her in a gush of clumsy words and emotions. Though he meant well, often times he ended up forcing a relationship to accelerate and be elevated to a higher level than it should have been for such a short period of time. These relationships quickly turned out to be flawed and just as quickly dissolved. They could not live up to the expectations of either person involved. As quickly as they had begun, they failed. They had been like some dazzling fireworks display that was beautiful for just a few brief moments and then there was no trace of it. After enduring what he considered his share of heartbreaks, daddy began to change his views on love. He gained a better knowledge of what it was that he essentially wanted out of a relationship.

Experience taught him what things he wanted and needed in a relationship as opposed to the superficial things of the past. His insistence on a fast pace gave way to patience, a realization that a solid foundation was needed for something permanent. After developing the areas within him that he knew needed work, daddy came to understand that the best relationships he had come to know matured gradually. According to his years of experience, friendship always seemed to be a good way to begin any lasting relationship.

Soon he restrained his youthful eagerness so that it would not destroy another relationship before it was given an opportunity to grow. He learned this same caution when he began potential relationships after his divorce. This caution was for my benefit as well as his since he knew whatever affected him would ultimately affect me.

He hoped to help me to avoid some of the mistakes he had made when he was a young man. For this reason, he wrote "My Quest for Love" as a way to illustrate the positive ways of establishing a sound relationship. It also serves to remind him, when he becomes impatient with people, of what he has learned to ensure the best chances that a solid relationship will continue.

My Quest for Love

Must my passion be stronger
than the sensible refrains
which conceal my true desire
to unleash emotions reins?
Is love to be a rival,
no friend of mine to be?
Then faintly it did signal,
slow your approach to me.
Through patience and humility
I've learned to slow my pace.
For true love is a journey
that must never be a race.

Chapter 12

Eternal Love

And He said to him, "You shall love the LORD your God with all your heart, and with all your soul, and with all your mind." This is the great and foremost commandment. And a second is like it, "You shall love your neighbor as yourself"
(Matthew 22:37–39).

O ne of the most difficult lessons we learn in life, which is similar to and may be related to that of love, may be dealing with members of the opposite sex. There are many complicated ways in which men and women interact and relate to one another. Not all of these relationships must be romantic.

Some men and women can be friends and confidants to each other, as was daddy with one of his best friends, a lady. They had known each other since they were young. The two of them, along with his sister, would go places and do things. Theirs was and continues to be a beautiful mixture of friendship and love. To this day he and this lady still make time to at least have lunch together in order to catch up on what is going on in their lives.

Daddy explained to me that he now loves this lady like a sister. Many times during his life, he had given serious thought of a future together with her, but they both decided that they did not want to spoil what they already had in a wonderful friendship. A romantic relationship might not have developed into anything yet it may have led to the end of their friendship, as they knew it. They could not expect to have a romance and go back to where they had been if their love affair for some reason did not work.

For years this lady remained a standard by which he dealt with every other woman in his life, and she was one of my role models as well. From their camaraderie Daddy found out that it was nice to have similar ideas and beliefs, a sense of humor, and the enjoyment of simply being in each other's company. In addition, she taught him how he could be at ease with a person of the opposite sex. They could each also offer a difference of opinion without fear of rejection or ridicule by the other person. This relationship taught him unconditional love and acceptance for who he was and how acceptance of one another related to their association.

That lady was a great source of strength for daddy in the troubled times immediately after his divorce. During his time of need, a time when most of his other friends disappeared, she showed all of us by her example, what it truly meant to be a good and loyal friend.

Daddy would always remind me how he believed that the interpersonal relationships we have are some of the most important parts of our lives. He also encouraged me to learn from the example of the two of them while I was still young. If I could get past the anxiety young people often feel when talking with the opposite sex, I would have a big lead on my peers as far as my social development was concerned. Later, his example of speaking with people would give me a sense of ease and self-assurance in life that became very helpful to me in many areas.

Daddy gave me an illustration of how I could overcome my bashfulness through an example from his life. He had the same trouble I was having in making friends when he was in high school because he was shy. His trick to overcoming his problem was to become the school photographer, thereby making friends by having them come to him. It seemed as if everyone in high school wanted to have his or her photo in the yearbook. Another good thing about his being behind the camera was just that: he felt as if he could hide behind it during those times when he felt less confident. Having the responsibility of being the yearbook photographer also placed him at all of the school sporting events and social activities even if he would not have normally attended such a function. This plan worked to help him come out of his shell as well as to make him a better photographer. He was also rewarded as he went on to get a scholarship to college for his work on the yearbook in photography.

By combining what I had learned from his relationship with that lady and his experience in overcoming bashfulness, I was able to deal with the opposite sex and with people in general on a much healthier level.

In his poem "Eternal Love," Daddy tells the woman that he wishes for her to have a wonderful life with or without him. He was confident that no matter what happened, nothing could end their friendship. She would always be an important part of his life, and he would continue to be an important part of hers.

He expresses a love that is pure, selfless, and eternal, one where only death could limit how much they care for one another. It is a wonderful example of platonic love between a man and a woman. I hope that someday I too shall be able to enjoy a relationship much like the one he had with his lady friend. I hope that I have learned from this how a person may be able to see beyond another's sex, age, or appearance to judge them for what they are on the inside. That, truly, is the best kind of relationship anyone could hope to possess.

Eternal Love

My happiness would not end were you to find another love.
Yet gone would be my best friend and the future I've dreamt of.
Within me there is no fear of the day you may depart.
For I know you will be here forever within my heart.
This pledge of love is not final, we both knew this from the start.
Our love can be eternal, not even when death do we part.

Chapter 13
A Lesson in Love

For God sees not as man sees, for man looks at the outward appearance,
but the LORD looks at the heart (1 Samuel 16:7).

Often in this hectic world, people get caught up in the rush of life. They don't take time to relax and to get back to the basic things that all of us need. Instead, they are too focused on the cares of everyday life: work, school, cars, homes, bills, not to mention trying to maintain the relationships of family, friends, and co-workers. It is easy to see how the simple pleasures that we all take for granted may get lost in the fast pace of our everyday lives. Sometimes, however, one must make time to see all of the joy life has to offer each of us. It can be found in even the simplest ways, as Daddy would show me whenever he found an opportunity.

Just after winning custody of me daddy took me to Disney World. It was going to be a celebration for just the two of us. We were having a great time until I needed to use the restroom. This news seemed to distress him as he got a bewildered look on his face. He had not considered what to do in the case of me having to go inside a public restroom alone. This was before the existence of family restrooms. Daddy stopped a lady who had two little girls my age and explained his dilemma. After she stopped laughing, she agreed to take me in the ladies' room with her and her girls. This was a humorous lesson. From that time on we always had an adult female with us just for such a challenge.

One of the most rewarding times I can remember sharing with daddy was when he took me along to volunteer at the Special Olympics. We spent almost the entire day at the stadium, from the opening ceremonies until the last award was presented to the athletes. At that time daddy was an Events Director for the Special Olympics in our area. Volunteering was one way he felt that he was able to give something back to the community and to show appreciation for the blessing of my good health. He was involved as a volunteer for several community interest groups, but the Special Olympics was always his favorite. It gave him an opportunity to spend time with young people, who I believe has always been a passion.

As we arrived at the stadium, my first job that day was to help him to organize the entire group for the opening of the ceremonies. Organizing everyone meant we would be lining up the athletes for the opening ceremonies, which had the athletes' parade in front of the grandstand before the games began. There were also athletes carrying a torch around the track to start the games. My favorite job came after the games started. I got to be what I like to call the "hugger." I would stand at the finish line and wait for each of the athletes I was working with to come across. When they did, I would give them a hug and tell them what a great job they had done regardless if they finished first or last. I also got to assist in presenting the medals to the winning athletes later that same day. I would hand the medals to the presenter who would then hang them around the athletes' necks. While I was working as a hugger, daddy was not far away working with a boy who had entered the standing long jump competition. The boy was rather short compared to some of the other boys competing. I watched as one of the taller athletes jumped 3 or 4 feet. I heard him ask the boy's teacher, who had brought him to the competition, if the boy was able to jump as far, and she said no. During practice the boy's first attempt was only about one and a half feet. It looked to me as though he was just taking a step forward and then bringing the other foot up beside the first. Then he showed the boy how to crouch and spring forward. He explained to the boy how he needed to pretend he was a frog. The boy practiced for several minutes before the competition actually began. When the time came for him to compete, he won first place and took home a gold medal! Daddy doesn't know this, but I saw a tear running down his cheek as he and the boy embraced after the competition. It was a very emotional time for everyone who knew that young man. The key thing for all of us to remember was not that the boy won but that he had done his best and displayed good sportsmanship. The boy also really seemed to enjoy himself in his efforts.

That night, as we relaxed on the porch, watching the stars move across the sky in their orbits above and smelling the orange blossoms that perfumed the summer night air, we reflected on what we each had learned from our wonderful experiences earlier that day. I spoke of how lovely it was that the athletes seemed to be concerned more about each other and what was happening at the time of their competition than they were about previous competitions, no matter if they had won or lost. Daddy agreed. He said we should all learn to live more in the present without having so much concern over what happened yesterday or what might happen tomorrow. *Come now, you who say, "Today or tomorrow we will go to such and such a city, and spend a year there and engage in business and make a profit." Yet you do not know what your life will be like tomorrow. You are just a vapor that appears for a little while and then vanishes away. Instead, you ought to say, "If the Lord wills, we will live and also do this or that,"* James 4:13–15. It is good to learn from yesterday but not to live in the past. By following the example of those athletes, we would all certainly learn to be happier. The other lesson that he pointed out was the unconditional love that all the athletes expressed for everyone they met. He told me that they love you for being you because they recognize that every individual is a special person.

That moment was beyond compare. Daddy rested there thinking of how beautiful all of it was. I felt happy just to be a part of this, and wanting to share this special time with him I reached my hand into his. Then I told him, "Daddy I love you." He said this scene of perfect serenity and peace grew much fuller and more perfect as we shared that moment together. He said for him, at that very moment, the stars shined a little brighter and the orange blossoms never smelled so sweet. He was so proud of me for the work I had done that day and the lessons I had learned. Along with the bonding, my work and personal growth had filled him with pride and joy.

The stars did seem to shine a little brighter for both of us that night, and the orange blossoms have never smelled as sweet to me again. Daddy always had a way of making me a part of those special times. He knew how to share the little things in life that make it unique. He taught me a great lesson in love by letting me watch how he interacted, respected, and loved people whom he had never met before as well as the love that he received in return. Some forms of love don't come naturally; they have to be learned. Being happy can be the same thing. It is this sort of idea, taking in happiness provided by the simple life that Daddy passed onto me and provides in the poem that he titled "A Lesson in Love."

A Lesson in Love

It was an evening in June
her smile brightened that dark night.
As the dimly lit half moon
Offered us its' balmy light.
The brush of a summer breeze
did relieve our every care.
As we sat back in our ease
Orange buds perfumed the air.
While the heavens were so clear
we could number every star.
Gazing toward them from here
they did not seem quite so far.
The evening was so very fine
what could I compare it to?
Then you placed your hand in mine
and whispered "Daddy I love you."

Chapter 14
Awaiting Her Return

All scripture is inspired by God and profitable for teaching, for reproof, for correction, for training in righteousness; that the man of God may be adequate, equipped for every good work (2 Timothy 3:16–17).

Good parents try their very best to give instructions to their children on how to live virtuous lives, knowing that as parents they cannot be there to watch over these children twenty-four hours a day. They must impart these lessons early in life and reinforce them along the way whenever possible hoping for a positive result.

Daddy loved and appreciated my childhood innocence as he watched the moral seeds he planted sprout and grow during my childhood. He, like many parents, knew a child reflects what the parents consider to be right and wrong, but only for a time. Eventually, that child will grow up to make moral decisions for themselves. At some point, children always manage to test their wings in the real world, using their limited knowledge of good and evil as a basic influence for living. Wondering how close they can get to a flame without getting burned is both fascinating and tempting. A good parent must try to balance the extremes of sheltering a child completely from harm, which doesn't give the child a chance to experience failure or get the bumps and bruises necessary for healthy growth. If parents only take a spectator approach in their parenting, allowing their child to do whatever the child pleases, it leads to disastrous results.

Children socialize, exchanging new ideas nearly every day. This means of communication is a part of their learning and growing. When children hear of and try to apply to their lives a new bad behavior based upon the ideas they share, it then becomes the parent's responsibility to point out and correct this new behavior before it can result in harm. If parents agree that children are exchanging these new ideas of bad behavior then why are parents not exchanging ideas, and successful methods they have found on stopping these bad behaviors? There is little doubt that bad behavior will lead a good child astray. This fall from grace can certainly be a nightmare for some parents. While some parents are confident in what will be the outcome of their parenting skills, worrying about the impact of bad influences on their children comes naturally.

My case of maturing was no different, as my daddy would come to find out. Soon I was to experience the growing pains that were associated with my own blossoming senses of morality and judgment.

My transition from elementary school to middle school was wrought with challenges. I went from a very comfortable, familiar environment to one that was new and daunting. Like most kids, I wanted to fit in and I followed some bad advice in my attempt. I received negative feedback from some close friends which hurt deeply. Instead of taking a constructive look and improving on immature behaviors: brattiness, snitching, being a know it all; I let the hurt sink in and cause me to feel that something was lacking with my personality. (Couple this incredible drop in self-esteem with starting two new middle schools within a year due to relocation where I would be learning new things like Algebra that was completely foreign to me.) I didn't want to gain further negative attention by asking for help, especially when asking for help was also unfamiliar to me.

These new stimulating events in my life would prove devastating to my schoolwork and my grades. Daddy tried a number of methods that should have gotten my attention, including positive reinforcement for good results. But the good results did not last for very long.

After all else failed, he used what I considered the ultimate weapon. He took away all of my privileges, including the television in my room, my stereo, the telephone, spending the night at my girlfriend's homes, and some others. Then he asked me to list all of the things that he had taken away and to explain how I would like to earn them back. He had me list them in their order of importance, with the number one answer being what I wanted to get back the most. After I had completed the list, he made a copy and handed it back. He explained that I would earn back the items I had listed in the reverse order in which I had listed them; I would get back the thing I want the most last!

This bit of psychology worked. My grades took a dramatic turn for the better. Daddy also showed me test results that I had scored in the top 90% of all the students my age in the entire state in every category. His method of discipline, coupled with him presenting me with my outstanding scholastic scores, helped my self-esteem, which had been suffering along with my grade point average.

One of the more humorous ways he used to nudge me back onto the road of acceptable behavior was by telling me that I had not always been an only child. I had an older brother, but he didn't behave. Whenever I was being a little mischievous in public, Daddy would say to me, "Your big brother used to do the same thing at your age." This message was our secret code that I needed to straighten up.

The poem titled "Awaiting Her Return" tells of a child's fall from innocence but how to make a return like mine. Parents who know their children are at home, where they are safer from most of the evil temptations of this world, can relate to this peace of mind. It is also something that I can turn to when I am in doubt of my decisions on matters, knowing that at least one other person believes in me and that I will make the right choices in life based upon what I was taught as a child. Even when I didn't make the right decisions, Daddy has always been there to help me back on the right path.

Awaiting Her Return

I fear for you when we are parted
because your youthful life has merely started.
The anguish I felt when you did fall
is known by parents one and all.
Though wisdom offered is often spurned
give heed to lessons that I have learned.
Weak spirits do burn with evil desire.
Array yourself in wholesome attire.
Flee those companions who may entice.
Do not yield my child to any vice.
Without exception be at your best.
Restoring one's virtue is a painful quest.
In knowing my child will be alright
slumber is welcome by me this night.

Chapter 15
The Virtuous Child

And now my daughter, do not fear, I will do for you whatever you ask, for all my people in the city know that you are a woman of virtue (Ruth 3:11).

Embarrassing moments are a part of my life that I wish I could have avoided. One of the most embarrassing moments of my childhood occurred when I was about eight years old. Daddy, Ma, and I were just returning home from church when we stopped at the grocery store for a few items. While we were at church it was mentioned that this day was Father's Day. That statement put me into a complete panic. How could I have forgotten this special day of the year? Because I had forgotten, I had no present or even a card to give him. I could not believe I let something like this happen! What a disaster this day was for me and soon would be for him if I could not make things right.

Thinking that I had come up with a clever plan to cover up my forgetfulness, I decided to buy something for him while we were at the grocery store. I asked for permission to go in alone to get something that he could pay for when I was done. Daddy replied, "There is no way I am letting you go inside by yourself young lady. I will, however, go inside with you and allow you to find what it is you are looking for by yourself, then I will meet you at the front of the store." This seemed like a good idea to both of us. While he went to pick up items on his list, Ma relaxed in a chair at the front of the store, waiting for me to return. I was now on a mission. What could I get at this grocery store to show him how much I loved him? As I went back to the front of the store to get a cart, Ma smiled at me. She said to me later, "You looked so cute pushing that big cart around." Grabbing a shopping cart, I proceeded down the first aisle as I began my shopping spree.

Daddy ran into a friend of his, and they began to talk. After a short time, I could see he had finished talking with his friend. From time to time, I would notice him just sort of checking on me to make sure I was okay. I began collecting things I thought would make good gifts. The first item I was to purchase was a Father's Day cake. The bakery department already had one made, so I asked them for that one. This seemed simple enough I thought. Next, I found an area of the store devoted to the new baseball franchise that had just come to our city. Both of us would need a T-shirt and a baseball cap. They also had a giant mug with the team logo on it, so naturally he needed to have one of those. From there I was able to find a section of the store that sold paperback books. I knew he would enjoy a book about Jurassic Park. After all, we both loved the movie. The next thing I did was to pick up several little items such as a "Happy Father's Day" coffee mug, a card, and some candy that we could enjoy together. After that I continued from one aisle to the next filling the cart with whatever goodies I thought he would enjoy. I just knew that this would be the best Father's Day of all time for him.

Having completed my shopping, I did the adult thing by getting in line with the other customers. When my turn came the cashier began totaling the items and asked me how I would be paying for this. I told her that I needed to get my Daddy. As I turned to find him, the line behind me parted allowing me to dash off in search of him. He was just finishing with the things he wanted to buy as I got to him. Actually, he had only picked up milk. When the two of us reached the cashier, my items had already been totaled and placed into bags. As he handed the cashier the milk, she asked if there was anything more. He replied, "No, I think we are done." At that point the cashier told him the total was *fifty-six* dollars and some change. Daddy's jaw dropped and his eyes got wide in disbelief and surprise! I was so scared. By now, there were quite a few people standing around us waiting to pay for their groceries. Most of them were already upset about the amount of time they had to wait while I searched for him and brought him back to pay for our items. At that point, if he had said anything about my purchases, it would really have caused a scene. He glanced at me out of the corner of his eye, and then without a word or further hesitation he took out his checkbook and paid for everything. I felt a little relieved, but I knew this was not to be the end of this matter. This Father's Day had gone from being bad to catastrophic.

As we were packing the bags into the car he said, "What in the world did you buy?" I nervously began confessing it all to him. How I had forgotten it was Father's Day and how all of those items were presents for him. He and Ma both broke out into uncontrollable laughter. He said for me not to feel too bad. This was as much his fault as mine since he had neglected to teach me about money. He agreed not to tell anyone about the incident at that time because of my embarrassment. But he did go on to say, in a joking fashion, my punishment would be postponed until I was married, when he would tell my husband to watch my spending habits. Later that day we took a few of the items back to the store for a refund.

At that time, money was very tight because he had spent about thirty thousand dollars during the custody battle, but he never complained or made me feel bad about the situation.

I will never forget how embarrassed I was, or how he came to my rescue by paying for all of that without scolding me in front of all the people in the store. It was shortly after this incident that he wrote "The Virtuous Child." In this poem he wanted to express how despite the turbulent times we had both recently experienced, as well as any that were to come, he remained proud of me, of who I was, who I was becoming and most of all how he would always love me. Daddy has been there for me when I needed him to protect me from people who may have tried to harm me as well as aiding me in the lessons of life that can be difficult for a child to bear alone. He has guided my growth by allowing me to have embarrassing moments, like the one in the store, without ridicule, as well as to make mistakes and learn from them without letting me fall too hard. This freedom has helped me to build character as well as developing my virtues.

Daddy was there to help me to grow strong. He never let the fact that our home was a "single parent household" become an excuse for us not to succeed in whatever either of us set out to do. He believed that if you think the best of people they usually live up to that level of expectation. He has always believed the best in me, and I have striven to be the best person that I can be as a result. When I read the poem, "The Virtuous Child," I am reminded of his love for me but it also reminds me of how he was and will always be my hero.

The Virtuous Child

When I ponder virtue and all it means to me,
my child, I think of you and what you hope to be.
Ideals in life inspire new goals for us to set.
Despite our foes' desire I know they will be met.
When you are in despair, and troubles seem to soar,
I will always be there, and they shall be no more.
Kids from homes now broken, might use that as a crutch.
But in our home it's spoken, I love you oh so much.
After all we've been through, those times which seemed so wild,
May this thought always comfort you, I'm blessed with you my child.

Chapter 16
Off You Go

*Train up a child in the way he should go, even when he is old
he will not depart from it (Proverbs 22:6).*

My first real job was as a bag person at one of the large retail grocery stores in our neighborhood. My family had known the store manager for several years, so it was no problem for me to talk him into giving me an opportunity to enter the job market as soon as I turned fourteen. As a matter of fact, he had already approached daddy earlier that year with the idea of my coming to work for him when I was old enough. It was exciting for me that he would approach us instead of the other way around. I thought that was pretty cool.

When my fourteenth birthday arrived, I was eager to get started. But daddy told both the store manager and me that I would have to wait until school was out for the summer before starting. This directive upset me at first; even if he was right, my thoughts had been about the cute guys who worked there, but school came first. Since summer vacation was only a few weeks away, I took an application home to have it ready the first chance I got. On the application, there were several places where I needed it to be explained what it was they wanted from me. Being grown-up might be harder than I first thought.

The next step after I had turned in my application was an interview, which gave me some cause for alarm since I had no idea what to expect and didn't think to ask daddy ahead of time. He took me up to the store, where we met with the manager. I was thinking to myself how I wished he would not leave me there in the office alone. It was a big step toward my growing up and doing things on my own. Daddy asked the manager how long he thought it would take and did some shopping to pass the time. The interview wasn't as bad as I had imagined. It was a little intimidating at first, until I read the questions. Some of the questions seemed silly. I didn't understand why he was asking me math questions when all I was being hired to do was put groceries into a plastic or paper bag.

The manager told me I had one more thing to do and that was to take a drug test. If I passed, I had the job. This test turned out to be the easiest part, even though at first it too scared me. I returned to the store with the paperwork indicating I had passed the drug screening, and the manager handed me a uniform shirt. "Wow!" I thought, "This is it"; I am about to begin my first job!

When the day came for me to start working, I wasn't nervous until we arrived at the store. Daddy wasn't sure if I wanted to just be dropped off in front of the store or if I wanted him to go inside with me. When he asked, I explained my sudden butterflies. He just smiled and parked the car. As we walked in, the manager met us. He handed me a name tag and told me I would be working for three hours. He and daddy talked for a few minutes while I was in the office watching a video on how to properly bag groceries. This video took about fifteen minutes, and by then daddy had gone home. Nervous would have been an understatement about my feelings when I realized I didn't know anyone there. As it turned out, the folks there were all very nice and helpful. Their encouragement made me feel extra special. I felt as if they really wanted and needed me to work there with them, not just that they were being nice.

Just before my three hours had ended, daddy showed up to see how I was doing. I was just returning from the parking lot where I had taken groceries out to a lady's car and helped her load them into her trunk. As daddy walked me back inside, he asked how my first day had gone. I told him it went great. As soon as we entered the store, I could see that a bag person was needed at the other end of the store. I ran across the store to get right on it. One of the assistant managers saw my enthusiasm. As he was talking to the manager, the assistant manager who saw me run to help told them both how impressed he was at my recognizing a bagger being needed and how I ran to correct the situation. This comment must have pleased the manager because he asked if I could work an extra hour and a half that day.

Because I was fourteen years old at that time, I was only allowed to work eleven hours a week. This didn't matter to me because I was now making my own money. Soon I had my first paycheck. Daddy and I had talked about how I should put half of my earnings into the bank and the rest could be mine to do with as I wished. It was at that point I began to really learn the value of money, but, more importantly, I had begun to grow from a child to a young adult. I felt a sense of responsibility and importance when I began working that I had not known before beginning that job.

It was about that time of my life that an important transformation occurred. My relationship with daddy had evolved. I was now an individual, a young adult. My complete dependence on him was lessening. No longer a child, I had reached a point where I had responsibilities and would be expected to answer for my actions. It was also at that time my daddy went from daddy to dad.

In the poem "Off you go" my dad describes his feelings about the time in our lives when he knew he had to release my hand to let me walk on my own. I will always be his little girl, his sunshine, and the treasure of his life.

Off You Go

Good-bye was all that I thought to say
as I paused to watch you walk away.
Not that I preferred to see you go
but feared your response if I said no.
What perfect words can be uttered yet
to face your future without regret.
Have I prepared you to face the world
so that your essence may be unfurled.
Know that I will always be here
as you begin this journey my dear.
No message is left from me to send
to help you to rise and to ascend.
But pausing to watch you walk away
Good-bye was all that I thought to say.

Chapter 17

Beginning My Own Life of Independence

Children, obey your parents in the Lord, for this is right. Honor your father and mother (which is the first commandment with a promise), so that it may be well with you, and that you may live long on the earth (Ephesians 6:1–4).

High school, college and then getting married were all challenging times to our relationship, with my wanting to be and eventually becoming an adult. We had some rough patches where dad and I seemed polarized. He still wanted to be my protector and advisor, but I wanted to have my complete independence. We both had some growing, adjusting, and learning during this phase of my life.

The next obstacle to our relationship was dad wanting us to hang out whenever possible, as we had done in the past. But for me, being married, having a full-time job, and working on my new house had become my new priorities. In addition, my husband and I were planning a family soon, and with the arrival of children, there would be even more demands on my time and energy, leaving little time to sleep much less socialize.

Dad had his own time demands with work, a new house, and taking care of Ma. Both of us were very busy with our responsibilities. It wasn't long until my relationship with dad grew even more strained, sometimes we would go for months seeing each other only briefly at church services. He didn't take my absence well, and we often argued over it. I'm certain with me being his only child and how he had devoted himself for years to my needs as well as the needs of our family, it was a role he felt comfortable filling. He did a wonderful job in that role.

I remember a fun time when I had some of my friends from college come to our house. One of them was looking through the movie collection we had when he came across a sealed package containing *Star Trek Bloopers*. None of my friends had ever seen those clips, and so my dad, without hesitation, opened the sealed package so that we could all watch it. He made the sacrifice of his collector's item without a second thought because he wanted me to be a gracious hostess.

But life has a way of changing circumstances, which create new roles or at least the roles we played can become altered in some way. It wasn't that I wanted him out of my life as if I had outgrown him, I just wanted him to realize our family dynamic had changed, and as a result we each had to make some changes. The ironic thing about it was by that time I no longer had a relationship with my mother, and now my lack of free time seemed to be pushing away my dad, the person who had done so much for me.

Was this to be the inevitable way in which families of today grow? Then, just as it seemed as if my life was going to be on one fixed course, it suddenly changed direction, and a new chapter in my life began; I found out I was going to be a mommy. God's timing was incredible.

What a wonderful time! I shared the news with dad, and later I shared with him the sonogram photos of my baby. Sharing with him these photos seemed to be the start of our bonding once again. A few months later, I mentioned to him how I wished I still had a relationship with my mother because I would have enjoyed having her throw me a baby shower, not for the presents; I just wanted family members there, having fun, and playing games. Dad said, "Let Ma and I do that for you." What an awesome gesture. I asked him if he would feel funny doing this girly thing, and he said, "Not at all, because I will have Ma take the lead for this party. I'm sure she'll have fun helping me." Later that same week, I spoke with Ma. She was very excited to be able to still do something special for me. Ma would be 84 years old about the time that my baby was due. Her physical health was not too bad, but by this time, she already had moderate to severe Alzheimer's, so there were some challenges for her.

Just prior to the baby shower we found out my baby was going to be a boy. That gave all of us who were involved in the planning of my shower the opportunity to plan a boy baby theme for my little prince.

The baby shower was a blast! Dad had researched many new games and fun ideas that we used at the party. Ma and dad made it a day I will never forget, with my family playing games and talking about old times as well as what I could expect with my new little one. All my family members assured me that I was going to be a wonderful mommy.

My dad came through for me again. He always has. Not very long after my son turned one year old, we learned we were to be blessed with a little girl.

At this point, it became obvious to both dad and I that our relationship had now grown from daddy-daughter to both of us being adults. He apologized for the hurt feelings which had developed due to our seeming to drift apart. He said that by him failing to communicate his feelings about our recent polarization he had failed to follow through on advice he gave me years ago as to how he believed in every healthy relationship there must be these three principles, good open communication, mutual respect, and honesty.

Afterwards, we were able to communicate more honestly and openly. I was able to present a different viewpoint in our relationship. I shared my thoughts on the possibility that at times he may have expected too much from people, and then as a result he became disappointed when they did not live up to his expectations. He was very open to my suggestion, and began working hard to change, and as a result he has made his relationships healthier.

Dad and I eventually came up with an idea for us to make time at least once every other month for us to hangout. We set ways in which we could seek a balance in our expectations. On occasion, he and I would have a daddy-daughter night out, but what he really came to enjoy even more was when my husband, children and I got together with him. Those times seemed to be extra special for all of us.

As my dad is growing old there are times now that he must rely on my husband and I to help him with things that come up. It's nice to be able to give back to him for all of the years he had been sacrificing so much for me.

He no longer writes poetry, so there isn't a poem to go with this chapter. Who knows, maybe one day he will write again if he has some new inspiration. But for now, I'm just enjoying, Special Moments with Daddy.

CPSIA information can be obtained
at www.ICGtesting.com
Printed in the USA
LVHW042330240821
696052LV00009B/266/J